Between Two Worlds

Written by Peter Rees
Illustrated by Spike Wademan

The Caribbean

Contents

Who Was Christopher Columbus? — 4

Voyage to Nowhere — 6

The Floating Islands — 8

Contact — 10

Kidnapped — 12

Cuba — 14

The Interpreter — 16

Shipwreck! — 18

Farewell to the Islands — 20

New World, Old World — 22

What If? — 24

Index — 24

Who Was Christopher Columbus?

Christopher Columbus was a merchant and sailor who lived in the 15th century. Back then, merchants were often adventurous people. They sometimes traveled far in search of new trading routes or markets.

Columbus is often said to have discovered America. However, he was really just one of the first Europeans to go there. People had already been living in America for thousands of years. Columbus was important because he brought the worlds of America and Europe together for the first time.

About 1451	August 3, 1492	October 12, 1492	October 14, 1492
Christopher Columbus is born in Genoa, Italy.	Columbus sets sail from Palos, Spain, looking for a sea route to Asia.	Columbus lands at Guanahaní in the Caribbean. He names the island San Salvador.	Columbus leaves Guanahaní with seven Taino Indians on board.

Setting the Scene

1492

In Columbus's day, people in Europe knew little about the rest of the world. Long-distance travel was difficult and dangerous, and few Europeans ventured farther than parts of Africa and into Asia.

Europeans were unaware that far to the west lay the continents of North and South America and the islands of the Caribbean Sea. The people who lived in those places had their own languages and ways of life. They knew nothing of other countries across the sea.

The two worlds were about to meet.

KEY

- - - -→ Columbus's first voyage

ATLANTIC OCEAN

BAHAMAS

CUBA

HAITI DOMINICAN REPUBLIC

Caribbean Sea

October 28, 1492	December 25, 1492	March 15, 1493	May 20, 1506
Columbus becomes the first European to visit Cuba.	Columbus is shipwrecked off the coast of Hispaniola.	Columbus arrives back in Spain.	Columbus dies at Valladolid in Spain.

Voyage to Nowhere

October 10, 1492

Christopher Columbus, captain of the Santa María, was worried. His crew was threatening to mutiny unless he turned his ship around and went home. For five weeks, steady winds had pushed them far across the Atlantic Ocean. Food and water supplies were running low, and Columbus could see the fear in the men's faces. But he couldn't stop now. All his calculations showed they had nearly reached their destination. He made a deal with the sailors—if they didn't sight land within three days, they would return to Spain.

mutiny to disobey orders from a ship's captain

Columbus was looking for a direct sea route from Europe to the rich markets of Asia. In late 1492, he sailed from Spain with three ships —the *Santa María*, the *Pinta*, and the *Niña*—and 90 men.

Columbus believed the world was smaller than it really is. By October, he was sure he was nearing China. He was, instead, about to become the first European to explore the Caribbean Sea.

In the 15th century, maps in Europe showed only those areas explored by Europeans. Sailors used stars, basic instruments, and guesswork to find their way across the oceans.

The Floating Islands

October 12, 1492

Quemi searched the blue water, his spear held high. Perhaps today would be lucky. Perhaps he would catch a caguama, the great sea turtle whose flesh would feed his family for many days. Even better, he might slay a fierce shark. Then all of Guanahaní would know he was a mighty hunter like his father, the chief.

Just then, Quemi heard a shout. Guani was standing in his canoe, pointing. Quemi stared. Beyond the lagoon moved three floating islands. They were made of wood, and they had great white wings. Quemi dropped his spear and paddled back to shore.

On October 12, 1492, Columbus arrived at an island in what is today known as the Bahamas. No one knows for sure which island it was. The people who lived on the island called their home Guanahaní. Although they often traveled between islands in wooden canoes, they had never before seen large ships like Columbus's.

The Guanahaní islanders' canoes were each carved from a single tree. This kind of canoe is called a dugout.

Contact

As Columbus and his landing party approached the island, they could see people watching from the shore. Columbus hoped they were friendly. Nevertheless, he was glad he had brought his sword.

On the beach, Columbus performed a special ceremony. He named the island San Salvador and claimed it for the King and Queen of Spain. Afterward, the people of the island stepped out of the forest and came forward to greet him. They were tall and strong. Many had brightly painted faces and bodies. They came in peace and traded gifts with the crew. Columbus noticed that some wore small pieces of gold jewelry.

> "They know nothing of weapons, for I showed them swords and they took them by the blade and cut themselves."
> —Columbus's journal

Like most Europeans of his time, Columbus didn't think about the rights and freedoms of the indigenous people he met. He decided to capture several of the friendly islanders and take them aboard the *Santa María*. He was impressed by their knowledge of the area and thought they would be useful guides on his voyage around the islands. He hoped they would lead him to the source of their gold.

This engraving shows the first meeting between Columbus and the people of the Caribbean.

indigenous belonging to an area

Kidnapped

In the morning, Quemi went to the beach to meet the strangers in their giant canoes. He brought parrots, spears, and cotton to trade for the visitors' colorful beads and other rare goods. Quemi smiled to himself. The beads would buy a lot on the other islands!

Something was wrong at the beach. There was Guani, struggling in the grip of two of the strangers. Suddenly Quemi was grabbed from behind, and his hands were tied. He was pushed into one of the smaller boats with Guani and some of the other islanders. They were taken to the big ships.

Columbus took seven members of the island population. He called them "Indians" because he believed he was near India. Actually, they were Taino people, whose ancestors had come from Asia at least 15,000 years before. For centuries, they had lived on the islands, fishing, trading, and tending crops, such as cassava and sweet potatoes.

The Taino lived in round huts called *bohíos*, which were made of wood and palm leaves.

Cuba

The Santa María sailed slowly up the wide river. From the deck, Columbus could see high mountains covered in jungle. The noisy calls of colorful birds came from the trees.

For the last ten days, Columbus had sailed from island to island, looking for gold and valuable spices. He had treated the captive Indians with kindness, and now they had guided him to this place. Columbus hoped there would be wealthy cities to trade with. Then he wouldn't go home empty-handed to the King and Queen of Spain!

kindness helping others

"This island is the most beautiful that eyes have seen."
—Columbus's journal

Although the Taino told him the great island was called Cuba, Columbus clung to his belief that he had arrived in Asia. He sent an expedition to the island to find the Chinese leader, the Great Khan. They took one of the Taino from Guanahaní with them as an interpreter.

Spices from Asia were a valuable commodity in Columbus's day.

interpreter someone who translates from one language to another

The Interpreter

Walking along, Quemi bit into a sweet, juicy pineapple. Mmmm! It was much better than the dry, salty food on the ship. Although he missed his family, things weren't so bad. Now that he had learned some of their language, the visitors respected him more. He helped them to speak with the local people. He had even shown the sailors how to make hammocks from old rope —more comfortable than the hard boards they slept on!

Although the chief called Columbus had promised he could go home soon, Quemi thought he might stay on board a while. Who knew what else he might learn?

respect to place a high value on something

16

The expedition came to a large village of about 1,000 people. The villagers welcomed the sailors warmly, seating them in special chairs called *duhos*. However, the villagers had few valuables to trade, so the sailors soon returned to the ships. Columbus decided to sail from Cuba and explore other islands.

Duhos were used by chiefs and other important people. They were often carved to look like people or animals.

Shipwreck!

Columbus woke with a start. A grinding noise shook the ship. In the darkness, the Santa María had run aground on rocks! Columbus went up to the deck. The ship was tilting, and it was hard to stand. Sailors ran in all directions. Some jumped into a boat and rowed away.

Columbus took charge. He told the men to drop the anchor and try to pull the Santa María off the rocks. It was too late. Water rushed in through holes in the wooden hull. Columbus had to think about the safety of his crew. He gave the order to abandon the ship.

When the *Santa María* ran aground, the *Pinta* was away on a voyage, and all the men did not fit on the *Niña*. So local Taino came in their canoes to help. Thirty-nine sailors stayed behind in what we now call Haiti. They made a fort using timber from the shipwreck. From the ship they also took weapons, seeds, and goods for trading. Unfortunately, the men were later killed during a confrontation with the people of the island.

This is believed by some to be the ship bell from the *Santa María*. It was found by divers off the coast of Portugal in 1994.

Farewell to the Islands

Quemi touched the collar of his shirt. The visitors' clothes he wore felt strange, although the cloth was soft. He would have to get used to them, since he would soon be living in Spain.

Behind Quemi, the last of the islands shrank on the horizon. Ahead of him lay adventure. He would go to this place called Europe. He would learn all he could and bring the knowledge back here, to his people. It was his responsibility as the son of a chief.

Quemi was looking forward to his adventure!

responsibility something we are trusted to do

When the ships reached Spain on March 15, 1493, the Taino aboard received a special welcome. Even King Ferdinand and Queen Isabella wanted to meet them! Later, all of the Taino took Spanish names. One, who had been especially helpful as an interpreter, was named Diego Colón, after Columbus's son.

This painting shows Columbus and the Taino meeting King Ferdinand and Queen Isabella on their return to Spain.

New World, Old World

Little is known about what happened to the Taino who sailed with Columbus. Most chose to return to the Caribbean with Columbus on his second voyage in 1493. One stayed in Spain but died soon after.

Columbus made three more voyages to the Caribbean. Others from Europe followed and settled the islands. They called these lands the "New World." However, to the Taino, who had lived there for centuries, it was an old world. Unfortunately, the European settlers brought with them diseases, slavery, and other problems. Before long, the Taino people and their peaceful culture were nearly wiped out.

New Ideas

The coming of European settlers to the "New World" nearly destroyed the cultures of the people who lived there. However, many of their words passed into European languages, and their foods became common on European tables. Before the voyages of Columbus, Europeans had never encountered:

- Vegetables such as potatoes, maize (corn), pumpkins, tomatoes, and chili peppers

- Some fruits, including pineapples, avocados, guavas, and papayas

- Peanuts, cashews, cocoa, and tobacco

- Many words, including *canoe, hurricane, barbecue,* and *chocolate*

- Hammocks, which soon became popular in ships everywhere

Left: In the United States, the second Monday in October is celebrated as Columbus Day.

What If?

When Columbus left Spain in August 1492, he was looking for a quicker route to Asia. He arrived at America completely by accident! Columbus still believed he had reached Asia and was most interested in finding gold, pearls, and other precious items.

What if you discovered a new continent? What about it would interest you most? Would it be learning about the people, the different kinds of animals and plants, or something else?

How did Christopher Columbus show determination in his voyage to and around the Caribbean?

Index

Asia	4–5, 7, 13, 15
Caribbean Sea	4–5, 7, 11, 22
Cuba	5, 14–15, 17
Guanahaní	4, 8–13, 15
Haiti	5, 19
navigation	7
Spain	4–7, 10, 14, 20–22
Taino	4, 13, 15, 19, 21–22

determination a drive to succeed